Museum Publications

Lace-Making in Hamilton — by Jessie H. Lochhead M.A.

Horse Drawn Vehicles in Hamilton Museum — by G. Walker

Hand-Loom Weaving in Hamilton and District — by G. Walker

Hamilton Palace, a photographic record — by G. Walker

Published by Hamilton District Libraries and Museum dept.
Chief Librarian C. Smith, A.L.A.

Fig. 1   The central section of the South Front, late 17th century

Hamilton Palace
a photographic record

Compiled and written by G. WALKER

Edited by C. SMITH, A.L.A., Chief Librarian

Fig. 2   The old North Front of Hamilton Palace, late 16th or early 17th century

Engraved in 1807

It is not known precisely where the family of Hamilton lived in Lanarkshire during the 13th and 14th centuries. Even the exact location of the "Orchard", their 15th century residence in Hamilton, is doubtful; though it is extremely probable that it was adjacent to the Collegiate Church in the Low Parks. Support for this theory is given by the evidence of nine feet thick foundation walls at the North East corner of the Palace. This suggests that an earlier "tower house" stood there, as the average thickness of the other walls was only three feet.

According to the date on a foundation stone the building or rebuilding of the house began in 1591. This house facing north was a substantial stone building three storeys high with steep sloping slated roofs. Side wings at right angles to the main building were connected to it by square towers. The engraving of the North Front (Fig. 2) drawn in 1807 shows this part before the 19th century rebuilding took place. On the right of this drawing some of the offices of the household are also shown. These included the kitchens, bakehouse, brewhouse, laundry and other workshops without which no large household at that time was complete. An engraving of Hamilton in the 1690's, which is in the Museum, shows the twin towers of the Palace with the church and buildings of the "Hietoun" clustered around them. The "Hietoun" was Muir Street, Castle Street and the area now occupied by the Ice Rink and entry to Strathclyde Park. In the foreground and on the right is the cultivated ground and houses of the Nethertoun. This area when it was being taken over for

4

gardens by Duchess Anne was called the fertile Nethertoun; it was well named as it is recorded that wheat was grown there in the 17th century.

No inventory or plan of the early building survives but this was the nucleus around which Duchess Anne and her husband Duke William decided to rebuild when times and their fortunes allowed. They consulted many authorities and inspected many examples of new work being done in Scotland and England before having the first draft plans drawn up in 1678 by the leading Scottish Architect, James Smith. These plans were to be altered many times before the final design evolved, but a start was made to the building in 1684 when a Glasgow builder was hired to erect a two-storey stable with a doorway wide enough to take a coach.

The general plan of procedure decided upon was to leave standing the original North Front, which had all the main rooms, and demolish and rebuild the side wings in stages, after which a new main entrance facing south would be erected. By 1701 the rebuilding was practically completed in spite of many difficulties and interruptions.

The South Front (Fig. 3) was a handsome structure in white freestone and the central section (Fig. 1) with its corinthian columns supporting a projecting entablature was truly elegant. Ornament was restrained and confined to the central section apart from the Duke's cypher over the doorways in the projecting wings.

Inside, the whole of the first floor of the centre block was occupied by a 120 feet long gallery (Figs. 4 and 5) wainscotted from floor to ceiling with great oak panels to accommodate the large family portraits. The Withdrawing and Dressing Rooms on the East Wing were similarly treated but the Great Dining Room, Drawing Room

Fig. 3   The South Front of Hamilton Palace, late 17th century

Photo Thos. Annand

Fig. 4 (*left*)   The 17th century Picture Gallery with the 19th century Throne Room at the far
end

Fig. 5 (*below*)   The entablature of the Picture Gallery

Fig. 6   The Dressing Room

Photo Country Life

and Bedchamber of the West Wing had only wainscotting to approximately 3 feet high. This was to allow for tapestry on the unbroken walls.

In the gallery could be seen portraits by Van Dyck, Kneller, Sir Joshua Reynolds, Lawrence and others. There were also, as the photograph shows, many rare and precious items, for instance the pair of Louis XIV Armoires of ebony inlaid with brass and tortoise-shell which are now in the Louvre and the pair of large globular Venetian vases encrusted with tortoise-shell inlaid with ivory and gold. The splendidly carved gilt table with the inlaid Pietra Dura marble top and the magnificent black marble fireplaces are also worthy of note.

In the Dressing Room (Fig. 6) the severity of the panelling was relieved by the superbly carved surrounds of the pictures, doors and fireplace. Here too could be seen a set of Queen Anne walnut chairs, the legs inlaid with gilt metal. The other oak panelled room shown is the Withdrawing Room (Fig. 7) where the woodcarving and the ceiling moulding enhanced each other.

The Great Dining Room (Figs. 8 and 9) with its three tiered bronze chandelier and Queen Anne furniture had an intricately patterned moulded ceiling. This ceiling like the others in the main rooms was executed by Thomas Alibourne, the master craftsman plasterer of that time. The woodcarving of this fireplace was by William Morgan as were all the other examples shown in the photographs. The supreme example of this carver's art, however, was the Great Staircase of oak (Fig. 10) which Smith erected in the west tower of the North Front. Each of the rails was from a single piece of oak and the ten panels showed children, animals, flowers and foliage intertwined with the monogram W. & A. for William and Anne.

The Duke and Duchess were very fond of this monogram and the Hamilton Arms Inn, now Hamilton District Museum, which was built during this period, had an intertwined WA over the rear door. This carving, however, was badly weathered and was covered over during the alterations.

Fig. 7   The Withdrawing Room, a late 17th century room furnished with Louis XVI gilt chairs and settee

Fig. 8 (*left*) The Great Dining Room of the 17th century rebuilding, the furniture is Queen Anne in walnut inlaid and mounted with gilt metal

Photo Country Life

Fig. 9 (*below*) Wm. Morgan's superb woodcarving in the Chimneypiece of the Great Dining Room

Photo Country Life

Fig. 10   The Oak Staircase shown in its 19th century site, it was originally in the West Tower
of the North Front

The other two large rooms in the west wing were the Drawing Room (Fig. 11) and the Bedchamber (Fig. 12). In the former only the mantelpiece surmounted by a magnificent crest and frieze is shown. The photograph of the latter, however, shows the rooms continuing through to the gallery and also a fine suite of Chippendale mahogany chairs and serpentine fronted table.

The plans of William and Anne were not confined to the building itself, the Duke took a keen interest in his gardens and the Duke and Duchess had always intended to landscape the grounds around the Palace. After the death of the Duke in 1694 the Duchess had a plan for the policies drawn up in 1708 by an ex-minister called Alexander Edward. This plan, copies of which can be seen in the Central Library

Fig. 11   The Chimneypiece in the Drawing Room

Reference Room and at the Museum, provided for the landscaping of the area from Bothwell Bridge to the High Parks. Owing to the death of Duchess Anne in 1716 and shortage of money this ambitious plan was never fully carried out. The Nethertoun was evacuated and demolished, however, and the separation of town and Palace had begun.

After the completion of building in the first two decades of the eighteenth century there was a cessation in building activity around the Palace. However, when the fifth Duke came of age in 1724, he had the architect William Adam prepare plans c. 1730 for a reconstruction of the North Front. William Adam, the father of the more famous Robert Adam, was at this time busily engaged with the building of Hamilton Parish Church and the ducal hunting lodge Chatelherault (Fig. 13). There is a tradition that Wm. Adam and not James Smith was the designer of the decoration of a suite of Palace rooms comprising the Duchess's Bedroom, Boudoir and Dressing Room. The evidence of the plasterwork in these rooms which is very similar to that of Chatelherault (Fig. 14) designed by Adam and executed by Thomas Clayton of Leith influences this belief. The new century, however, had brought about a change in the style of decoration. Light plaster scrolls instead of heavy woodcarving was now the fashion, and either Smith or Adam could have used the new forms.

Fig. 12   The Bedchamber in the 17th century West Wing looking through the Drawing and Dining Rooms to the Gallery

Photo Country Life

Fig. 13   Chatelherault in 1962, 18th century hunting lodge in the High Parks designed by
Wm. Adam

Photo G. Walker

Fig. 14   Part of the plaster ceiling and cornice of the Duke's apartment in Chatelherault,
plasterer Thos. Clayton of Leith. Photographed in 1962

Photo G. Walker

Fig. 15 (*left*) The Duchess's Bedroom, late 17th or early 18th century, furnished with mid 18th century French gilt chairs and a blue and gold Brussels carpet. The bed is carved and gilded "tulip" wood

Fig. 16 (*below*) The fireplace corner in the Duchess's Bedroom showing the plasterwork which was probably designed by Wm. Adam and executed by Clayton. The painting inset in the panel is a view of the Thames by Scott

c.

Fig. 17 A corner of the Duchess's Dressing Room with a portrait of Marie, Princess of Baden, Duchess of Hamilton

These new forms show up to advantage the magnificent carved gilt bed, the Louis XVI gilt chairs and the Romney painting of the Misses Beckford in the Duchess's Bedroom (Figs. 15 and 16). They also enhance the Rock Crystal chandelier, Sheraton satinwood tables and collection of miniatures in the Dressing Room (Fig. 17). The third room of this suite, the Boudoir (Figs. 18 and 19), is a delightful example of eighteenth century design.

The death of the fifth Duke in 1743 and possibly the cost postponed the alterations to the North Front, but the plan of William Adam was used as the basis for rebuilding by a later Duke. Large scale building may have stopped but in a house of that size maintenance could not. There were alterations and improvements to be made and the journals of John Burrel, Chamberlain to the Duke of Hamilton for most of the second half of the eighteenth century, are very detailed. Everything was carefully estimated and costed from the price of paint for the Palace exterior at approximately 8d per sq. yd. to the price of beef for the staff at $2\frac{1}{2}$d per pound. One of the alterations in 1780 was a new chimney-piece costing £8.6.4 for the Stonehall which was situated under the Picture Gallery, but another and more important improvement in that year was to bring a water supply into the building. Up to that time the water required for the Palace was drawn from wells in the vicinity of the courtyard and carried to where it was needed. This first piped water supply was taken from the lade to Hamilton Mill which drew its water from the Cadzow and Butter Burns and entailed the laying of 520 yards of 2″ bore pipe at eight shillings per yard to a reservoir in the Palace courtyard. One hundred and seven yards of 1″ bore lead pipe, two large lead cisterns, brass taps, cocks, sinks, etc. were required to give a water supply to the kitchen, scullery, butler's pantry, washhouse and coachhouse. A Glasgow plumber named George Douglas was asked to estimate and then install the system, which he did at a cost of two hundred and thirty one pounds.

Fig. 17a Armchair, carved and gilt, upholstered with tapestry, French Louis XVI

Photo Country Life

Mr. Douglas was also asked in 1779 to estimate for the installation of a water closet to be located under the Great Staircase and this he was able to do even though the first patent for a W/C was only taken out in 1775. The estimate dated December 31st, 1781 reads "Estimate of the expense of a water closet below the Great Staircase of the Palace, to double ball water closet including soil pipe, stink trap and work setting up £20". A footnote added that for an additional £10 another seat and apartment could be added.

19

Fig. 19 (*above*)   The Chimneypiece in the Duchess's Boudoir

Fig. 18 (*left*)   The Duchess's Boudoir showing superb 18th century plasterwork

Photo Country Life

Fig. 20   The 19th century North Front and Office Court of Hamilton Palace, architect David Hamilton

22

The later account revealed that only a single seat was installed but after this plumbing costs were a regular feature of the accounts as various additions to the water supply were made.

Local tradesmen were used whenever possible for repairs and additions and even for furniture making. For instance the local wright, Gavin Rowat, as well as constructing and setting up windows, doors, stairs and walls, supplied in 1777 various pieces of furniture e.g. an oak table 9′ 6″ × 2′ with three leaves, six drawers and locks for £2.10s. However, specialists like the plasterer Thomas Clayton were employed in 1782 to decorate the Stonehall, Staircase, Bedroom and Vestibule.

Whether this bedroom is the one shown in Figs. 15 and 16 and referred to earlier

Fig. 25 (overleaf) The Drawing Room before the sale of 1882

Photo Thos. Annand

Fig. 21 (below) The Portico of the North Front

Photo Country Life

Fig. 22 The Black Marble Staircase showing the stairs branching right and left to the top landing. The marble topped side table is reputed to be by Wm. Kent, the early 18th century artist and sculptor

Photo Country Life

Fig. 23   The top of the Marble Staircase showing the vaulted roof and a portrait of Empress
Eugenie of France by F. Winterhalter

Fig. 24 The Grand Entrance Hall with a bronze bust of Alexander 10th Duke and a suite of carved mahogany armchairs, Empire style

Photo Country Life

Fig. 24a (*right*) A mahogany armchair, English, late Empire style, c. 1820

Photo Country Life

Fig. 26   The Hamilton Library looking through to the Drawing Room and Entrance Hall

Fig. 27 The new Dining Room with a fireplace of white marble and paintings by Van Dyck

cannot be determined as the room's location is not specified. We only know that 86 feet of enriched entablature at 3/- per foot was supplied and that it was a continuation of work already done. The entablature in this instance is the cornice and frieze of the room. Thomas Clayton was one of the foremost craftsmen plasterers of his day and his work can still be seen in Blair Castle in Perthshire, Hopetoun House in East Lothian and Holyroodhouse in Edinburgh. This did not, however, stop the Duke complaining about his high prices in an account totalling £285.

Various other improvements continued but the most notable was the gradual acquiring of the land around the Palace by purchase, exchange or termination of leases. The reason for this was to obtain space for rebuilding and landscaping the area around the Palace. By 1819 when the tenth Duke came of age most of the land required was in the Hamilton estates and Duke Alexander was able to proceed with his grandiose plans.

The Duke, a noted art collector himself, had married Susan, daughter of William Beckford, who had spent his father's millions in acquiring a vast collection of valuable books, pictures and ornaments. The Duke, no doubt influenced by his father-in-law, determined that a residence worthy of the family position should be erected. He employed David Hamilton of Glasgow as architect but he himself was the chief designer and Wm. Adam's plan was the basis from which they worked.

The old North Front was demolished and in its place was erected the 264 feet long edifice shown on Fig. 20. The central portion or portico (Fig. 21) consisted of a double row of Corinthian columns each 25 feet high and 3 feet 3 inches in diameter.

Fig. 28 The Tribune

Photo Lafayette

Fig. 29   The Throne Room

Fig. 30   "Daniel in the Lion's Den" by Sir Peter Paul Rubens

These were each made from a single block of stone and brought from the quarry at Dalserf in a specially made vehicle drawn by thirty horses. Entry could either be made to the first floor via the Portico steps or by doorways under the steps to the Egyptian Hall on the ground floor. The main entrance to this hall, which was the 17th-century Stone Hall remodelled and extended, was by the main entrance on the South Front. From the hall a passage led to the foot of the Marble Staircase (Fig. 22) and this view shows the two colossal bronze figures by Soya of Paris which appeared to support the upper landing. The staircase and landings were constructed throughout of black Galway marble, a favourite material of the tenth Duke.

The plans of the ground and first floors illustrated on the inside of the front cover will assist in locating the rooms mentioned but unfortunately some of the rooms were renamed after the 19th century rebuilding. For instance the Withdrawing Room became the Music Room, the 18th century Dining Room became the Breakfast Room and the Drawing Room became the old State Drawing Room.

From the top of the Marble Staircase (Fig. 23) the way to the tapestry rooms was through the Grand Entrance Hall (Fig. 24). This 54 feet square hall was paved with Sienna and black marble and was 42 feet high, and was originally illuminated by gaslight from four pillar lamps, two of which can be seen beside the fireplace. The first of the tapestry rooms was the Drawing Room (Fig. 25), unfortunately, this is the only room we can show with the tapestries in place. Below the rare Italian tapestries is shown a Buhl commode with a top of green malachite and a suite of Louis XVI gilt chairs covered in Gobelin tapestry.

Adjacent to the Drawing Room was the Hamilton Library (Fig. 26) sumptuously furnished with sofas and armchairs covered with tapestry and lit by a gilt bronze rock crystal chandelier hanging from the panelled ceiling. The new Dining Room

Fig. 31   The Picture Gallery in 1919

(Fig. 27), the spacious room nearest to the library, was built to cope with large dinner parties and the mahogany table could extend to 32 feet by 6 feet. Between this room and the picture gallery was the Tribune (Fig. 28) and at the far end of the gallery was the Throne Room (Fig. 29). Duke Alexander had been Ambassador to Russia and had brought home the throne he used in St. Petersburg to be installed in the gallery.

Most of the paintings hung in the gallery were portraits but one notable exception was "Daniel in the Lion's Den" by Sir Peter Paul Rubens (Fig. 30). This photograph was taken for Country Life magazine in 1919 and in this view of the gallery (Fig. 31) the painting can be seen between the fireplaces. Sold in 1882 for £5,145, the work was bought back three years later for £2,100 and resold in 1919 for £2,520. It is now in the National Gallery of Washington, U.S.A.

Also on the first floor was the Billiard Room (Fig. 32) and the Beckford Library (Fig. 33). The Library was a large T shaped room built on the South Front to house the rare books and art objects bequeathed to the tenth Duke and Duchess by her father. The library was on the first floor and access was via the old state apartments, alternatively the room could be reached from the ground floor by ascending the oak staircase. This staircase had been moved to a position near the Kitchen Court when the West Tower was demolished in the 19th century alterations.

Whilst the building was being remodelled and the Mausoleum built, grand avenues of trees were being replanted in the grounds (Fig. 34). The last houses of the town which were adjacent to the Palace were pulled down and the wall around the policies completed. This wall which stretched from Bothwell Bridge to Motherwell Bridge had three main entrances, Bothwell Bridge, Almada Street and Edinburgh Road. There was also in Motherwell Road a stretch of giant iron railings which were

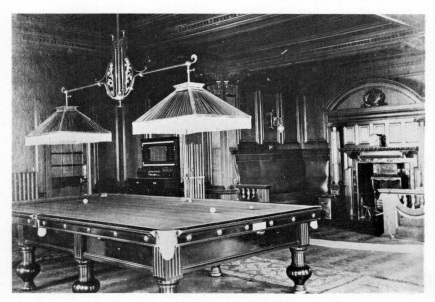

Fig. 32   The Billiard Room

Fig. 33   The Beckford Library with a portrait of Wm. Beckford by Romney

Photo Lafayette

Fig. 34   The view from the Palace looking North

Photo Thos. Annand

cast at Shotts Iron Works. Fortunately some of the railings were saved and are now erected in front of the College of Education in Bothwell Road.

Among other improvements the Duke completed was a reservoir at Chatelherault to provide a purer water supply for the Palace, a private gasworks at Smithycroft and the installation of gas lighting in the Palace and its vicinity. Alexander died in 1852 but the debts incurred by the rebuilding and art purchases had left a heavy load on the estates. As these debts were increased by his successors, it was decided to sell off most of the art treasures.

The sale took place at Christies salerooms, London in July 1882, lasted for 17 days and raised £397,562. This would probably be between four and five million pounds at today's values and Duke Alexander has never been given credit for his skill and acumen as an art collector. It was a tragedy for Scotland that his collection was dispersed and now graces some of the finest galleries in the world. Apart from the artistic value there was also the financial to consider. If we compare the sale prices with the inventory values of 1835, which were presumably entered at cost, we find that practically every item has appreciated substantially. Paintings, for instance, realised up to five times their book value and the best examples of French decorative furniture brought as much as twenty times their quoted price. A priced catalogue, which can be seen on request in the Central Reference Library, gives some idea of the scope of the collection. The engravings in this catalogue are delightful and all the examples reproduced in the booklet are from this source.

After the sale the Palace continued to be used by the Hamilton family but somewhat less frequently. Now that travelling was easier the Hamilton family kept only a skeleton staff in their large houses. Their personal staff and bulk of their

Fig. 35   The reception for King George V and Queen Mary at Hamilton Palace in 1914

Fig. 36   The Drawing Room adjoining the Hamilton Library c. 1890, showing a Flemish marquetry cabinet and a fine suite of gilt furniture with cabriole legs and ball and claw feet, c. 1730

Photo Lafayette

Fig. 37 (*above*)   An architect's drawing for the White and Gold Staircase

Fig. 38 (*below*)   The Palace Railings and wall on the road to Motherwell, 1962

Fig. 39   The bedroom in the Princess Suite with a carved and gilded Parisian bed hung with a canopy of green satin damask

Photo Thos. Annand

Fig. 40 (*above*) The Breakfast Room, originally the 17th cent. Dining Room, with a portrait of the Countess of Coventry (nee Maria Gunning) by Gavin Hamilton

Photo Lafayette

Fig. 41 The Drawing Room c. 1890 with a French marquetry writing table and French gilt armchairs and sofa

Photo Lafayette

Fig. 42　Two portraits of William 11th Duke, as a child by Sir H. Raeburn and as a boy by R. Buckner, in a corner of the Duchess's suite

Photo Lafayette

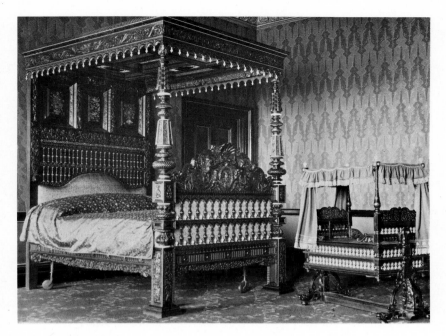

Fig. 43　An Indo–Portuguese bedstead of ebony decorated with ivory, mother-of-pearl and tortoise-shell and a matching child's cradle

Photo Country Life

Fig. 44　A corner of the Duchess's Drawing Room with portrait of the Grand Duchess of Baden

Photo Lafayette

Fig. 45   One of a pair of Louis XIV Armoires made by Buhl of ebony inlaid with brass, tortoise-shell and ormulu. The pair were sold in the 1882 sale for £12,075 and are now in the Louvre, Paris

Fig. 46   A Louis XVI Secretaire of ebony, lacquer and ormulu made for Marie Antoinette
whose monogram is on the frieze. It was sold for £9,450 in 1882

Fig. 47   A Louis XVI Commode made for Marie Antoinette by Reisener, this piece with a
companion secretaire was sold in 1882 for £4,305 and £4,620 respectively. They are now in the
Frick collection, New York, U.S.A.

servants came to Hamilton only when they were in residence. Large scale entertaining was still done on occasions like the reception of King George V and Queen Mary in 1914 (Fig. 35).

However, the upkeep of a house of this size was a burden on the estates and, though there was no coal workings under the Palace at this time, the whole area round about was subsiding. The fourteenth Duke and Duchess were advised therefore to evacuate the Palace and move to a smaller house which could be more easily managed. The house chosen was Dungavel five miles south of Strathaven.

The ensuing sale which was again at Christies raised record prices. For example a Romney painting of the Misses Beckford, see Fig. 15, for which the painter received £105 realised £54,600, a record price at that time for a painting, and a Reynolds of "Alexander the tenth Duke as a boy" brought £13,125. Catalogues of this sale can also be seen on request at the Central Reference Library.

Shortly after the sales had taken place in London and in Hamilton, it was decided by the Hamilton Trustees to demolish the Palace and in 1922 the grounds in the Low Parks were sold to Hamilton Town Council. Demolishers then did not have the equipment or expertise that they now have and prices for salvaged materials were low. One of the demolishers, for instance, was offered two shillings and sixpence ($12\frac{1}{2}$p.) for the magnificent chandelier in the dining room. The task took nearly eight years to complete and during this time some homeless families were housed there. Last to go was the Office Court which was used as a changing room by the football teams playing in the new recreation grounds.

The final episode in the saga of the Palace took place in 1974 when a bulldozer, working in the new Regional Strathclyde Park, dislodged a stone and exposed what was thought at first to be another well. Examination, however, revealed that the heavy earth-moving machines had been running backwards and forwards over the vaulted roofs of the Palace cellars. For safety's sake the foundations had all to be exposed, the cellar roofs collapsed and everything covered over once more. The football and rugby pitches, which lie between the new "Hamilton Palace Pavilion" and the slip road to Motherwell, now cover all that is left of Hamilton Palace.

1806

Fig. 48   A very fine Louis XV parquetry Commode with shaped front and ends, mounted with massive ormulu chasing, sold for £6,427 in 1882

46

BIBLIOGRAPHY

The Days of Duchess Anne   *R.K. Marshall*

Hamilton Palace (published in Country Life)   *H. Avray Tipping*

Hamilton Directory of 1855/56   *J. Muir*

Hamilton Directory of 1879   *W. Naismith*

The journals of John Burrel and the Hamilton Palace Inventories in the Hamilton Collection of the Central Reference Library.

488

THE PHOTOGRAPHS

The views were selected and copied by the Museum staff from prints in the Photographic Collection and albums in the Central Reference Library. The earliest album is that of Thos. Annand who began his photographic career in Hamilton. His photographs were taken sometime before the sale of 1882 when Duke Alexander's art collection was still in the Palace. Students of photography will appreciate that indoor photographs of this quality and of this period are rare indeed.

Judging by the furnishings, the views in Lafayette's album must have been taken during the late Victorian period. They were certainly photographed after the 1882 sale, probably around the turn of the century, and whilst they are not of so high a quality they illustrate some of the other rooms.

When "Country Life" magazine published their series of articles on Hamilton Palace during the summer of 1919, it had already been decided to close down and demolish the building. We are indebted to Messrs Country Life Ltd., for the use of their splendid photographs and also to the many individuals who have donated prints to the Museum, some of these prints are reproduced in this booklet.

Hamilton District Museum

129 Muir Street Hamilton

Hours of opening:
Monday to Friday—10 a.m. – 12 noon and 1 p.m. – 5 p.m.
Saturdays—10 a.m. – 5 p.m.
Sundays closed

HOW TO GET THERE...

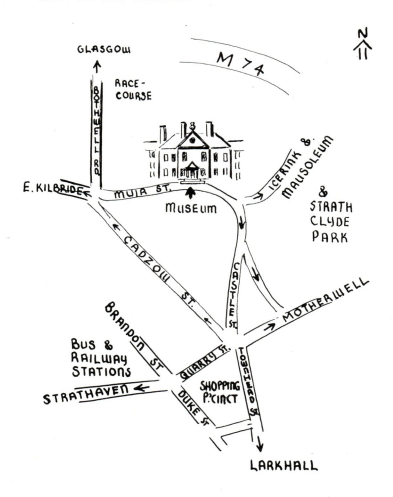